Dedicated to
Leslie, Andy and Marni for tolerating our passion to collect -
and pretending to enjoy it!

with a coffin-shaped wooden fiddle case, carved with stars, an eagle, and playing cards (pp. 53). The instrument he takes out is even more extravagant. It is made of 41 different woods, and the scroll is a coiling snake swallowing a frog. Imagine how the fiddler must have played! Or perhaps Lew Quigg, who made it, just wanted to give the fiddler something interesting to look at while he worked his way through those jigs and reels.

Because so many works of outsider and folk art are anonymous or beyond the accepted canons of taste, collectors of this material constantly have to face up to their insecurities. Especially when prices seem incomprehensible. It's axiomatic, however, that you never regret things you buy, only those you don't. We have learned to trust ourselves and a few people whose opinions we value. Call it confidence or foolhardiness, it has often paid off. One of the most eccentric objects in our collection is a desk made in 1878 in Sussex, New Jersey, by G.P. Ailers (pp. 54, 55), who continued to work on it until he died. It is in the Adirondack style, but so extreme, so obsessive, it seems alive. We needed to make sure we could live with it and that it wouldn't overwhelm the rest of our collection. So we tried it in our house, and strangely enough it fit right in. In fact, it became one of our most treasured pieces. We have never put things in warehouses. They need to be lived with and experienced, so everything we acquire has to pass the "house test".

Our desire to know as much as we can about the stories these objects tell has led us, whenever possible, to the artists themselves. We were never able to meet Cal and Ruby Black or Bill Traylor or other artists we admire, but we did have the pleasure of visiting Thornton Dial in Alabama and watching him work. When he had his first major exhibition in New York in 1992, we arranged a cocktail party at our home in Westchester so he could see how his work looked on the wall. His presence, his Southern diffidence, was unforgettable. We had glimpses of the living person. Recently we acquired one of his most unusual pictures, *Flowers of the Blue Things (pp.30)*, which he created after a visit to the Museum of Modern Art and hours spent in front of Monet's Water Lilies. We think of Dial's painting as our Monet. And when we look at it, we can almost see him at work on it, pasting down the flowers, with the image of Monet's painting in his mind's eye.

Our desire to see art more clearly, choose with greater discrimination, and make our collection an expression of our own growth has led us to meet many other remarkable people. This has been the greatest unexpected benefit of our collecting adventure. Jay Johnson and Reubens Teles, who understood our passion and steered me to Robert Bishop, gave us the gift of our beginning. The Clokeys started us collecting anniversary tin, and June Lambert fed this obsession. Phyllis

Elijah Pierce **Jonah and the Fish** 1949, carved and painted wood relief with glitter, 15 1/4"H x 28 1/2"W x 1"D
(following page) Morton Bartlett **Waving Girl** (detail) ca. 1950-60, carved and painted plaster with fiber hair, 32 1/4"H x 6"W x 4"D

Kind, Ron Jagger, John Ollman, Luise Ross, Marion Harris, Aarne Anton, Shari Cavin, and Randall Morris introduced us to the work of the masters within this field. Carl Hammer offered passion and friendship. Joel and Kate Kopp and Candace Browne led us to musical instruments and to the unique quilt in our collection. Sanford Smith, the impresario of art and antique shows, directed us to the "best pieces". And Barbara Strand and Daniel Toepfer have enhanced Gael's Kitsch Room *(pp. 93)*, an ongoing project involving the creation of a "kitsch" environment.

Special thanks to Marni Giannotti for her assistance on the photography shoot. Additional thanks to Gerard C. Wertkin and the Museum of American Folk Art, to Laura Wiley, William Arnett, and to Peter Neil at the South Street Seaport Museum for the opportunity to guest curate *Sacred Waters: 20th Century Outsiders and the Sea.*

Fred Giampietro has played a role that is too pervasive to define. As a dealer and advisor, he has been instrumental in our acquiring major works. But the best way to describe his influence is to say that he has given us a sense of the responsibilities involved in serious collecting.   He taught us the basic lesson that quality is more important than quantity.

We met Roger Ricco and Frank Maresca at an antique show when a red violin case with a profile of its maker drew us to their booth. They have been pivotal in our evolution because they have done what the best dealers do: pushed us to push the envelope of our taste and imagination. They have opened doors to new and more challenging aesthetic worlds, to objects capable of very different ways of telling. In the beginning, we never imagined we could aspire to develop the taste they possess, at once raw and sophisticated. But over time, their influence gave us an eye for unique work, and when we acquire a piece now, we still measure it by their stamp of approval.

The objects in this collection have made a place in our home and in our lives. It is our hope that by exhibiting them, they may also make a place in other people's lives and inspire them with the stories they tell.

Gael and Michael Mendelsohn
2000

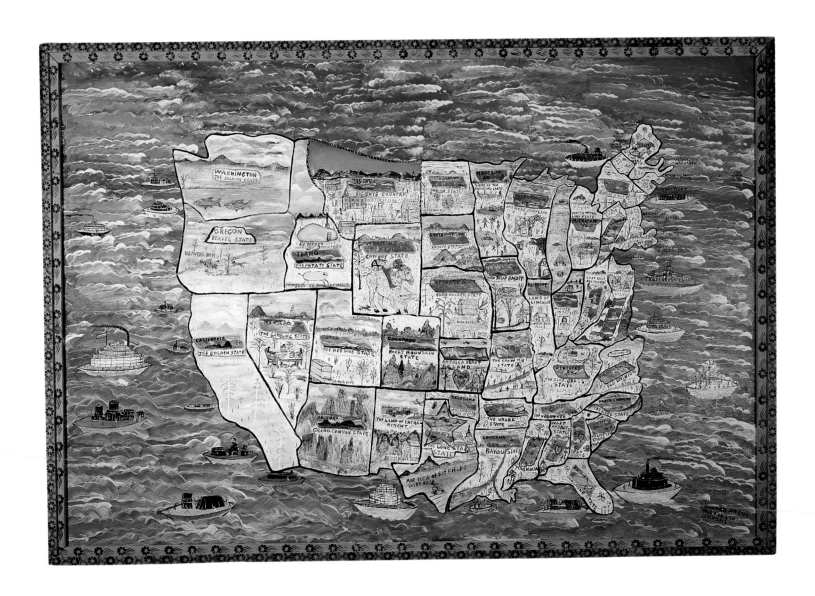

Howard Finster **The Story Map** 1976, enamel on plywood, 41 1/2"H x59 1/2"W

Calvin Black **Possum Trot Fantasy Theatre Dolls** ca. 1955-72, wood, fabric and metal with polychrome
Me Big Chief (left): 60 1/4"H x 13"W x 6"D; *Jan (center):* 36 1/2"H x 9"W x 6"D; *Outdoor Figure (right):* 51"H x 15"W x 6"D

(right) **Bust of a Man with Crossed Arms** ca. 1830-50, wood with polychrome, 14"H. Probably made by followers of
William Miller (1821-849), known as Millerites, who believed the world would come to an end in 1844.

Joe Mullet **Carving of a Man** early 20th C., limestone, 26"H x 13 1/2"W x 7"D
(*left*) Stanley Papio **Bust of a Woman** ca. 1959, welded chrome-steel car bumpers, 25"H x 25"W x 8"D

William Hawkins **Tasmanian Tiger #3** 1989, enamel and mixed media on Masonite, 48"H x 8"W x 4"D

William Hawkins **Juke Box** 1987, enamel and mixed media on Masonite, 60"H x 48"W x 5"D

39

Sam Doyle **Uncle Remus** 1982, enamel on window shade, 72"H x 35"W

Sam Doyle **First Football Game** ca. 1978-81, enamel on tin, 49"H x 28"W

41

Cecil B. White **Scenes from American Life** ca. 1925, mixed fabrics, 77"H x 66"W
(right) detail

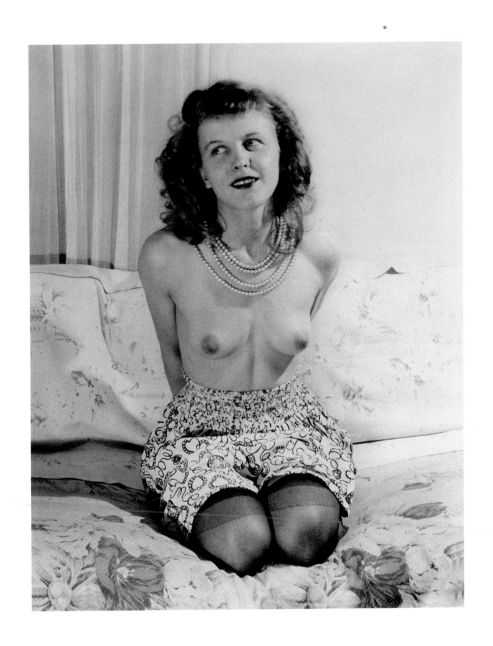

Eugene Von Bruenchenhein **Portrait of the Artist's Wife** ca. 1945-51, hand-colored vintage gelatin silver print, 8"W x 10"H

45

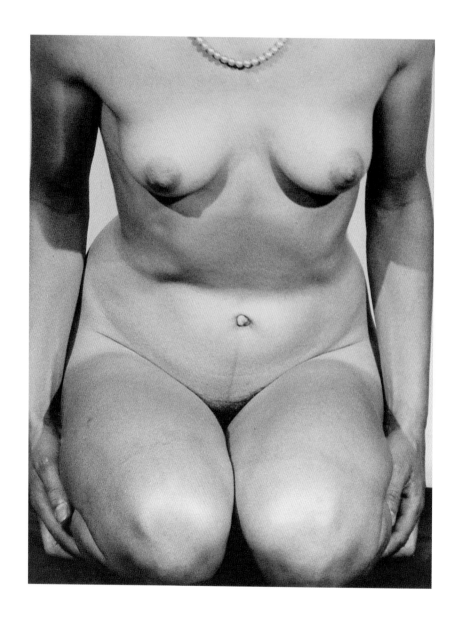

Eugene Von Bruenchenhein **Portrait of the Artist's Wife** ca. 1940s, vintage gelatin silver print, 8"W x 10"H

Eugene Von Bruenchenhein **Portrait of the Artist's Wife** ca. 1945-51, toned vintage gelatin silver print, 8"W x 10"H

47

Eugene Von Bruenchenhein **No. 769** 1958, oil on board, 24"H x 24"W

Eugene Von Bruenchenhein **No. 866** 1960, oil on board, 21 3/4"H x 24"W

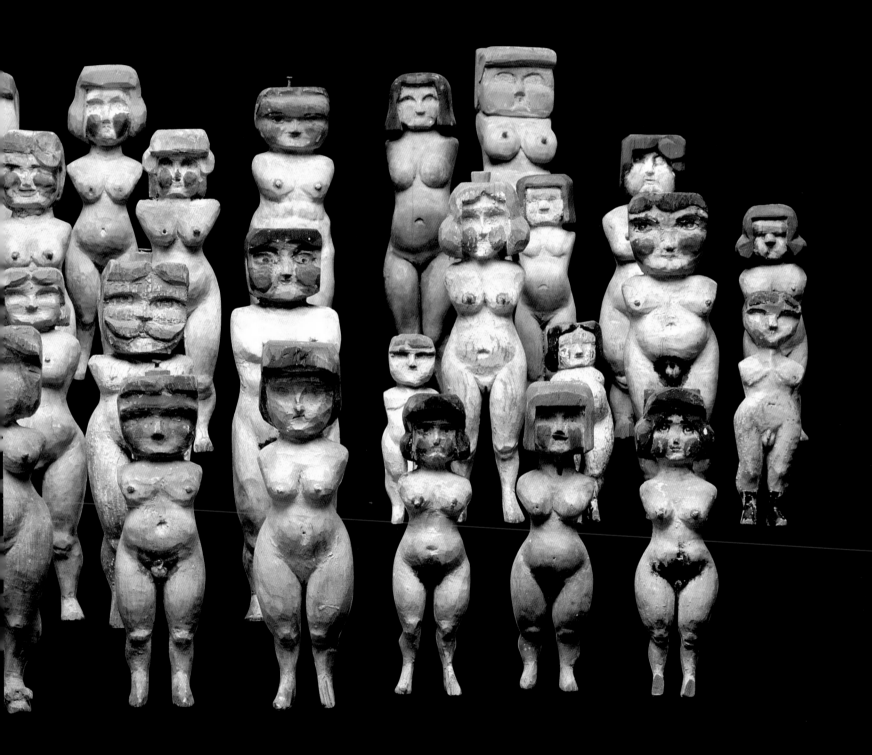

Joe Henry Hunley **Violin** ca. 1930-40, carved wood with polychrome, 31"H x 12"W x 4"D
(*previous page*) **Woodbridge Figures** ca. 1920-40, wood with polychrome, ranging in size from 4 1/2"H to 7 3/4"H

Anniversary Tin Bouquet 1899, tin, 14 1/2"H x 6 1/2"W x 6"D

Henry Darger **Untitled (At Gennie Richie)** ca. 1950-60, watercolor and ink on paper, 23"H x 107 1/4"W
(*top*) Side A (*bottom*) Side B (*overleaf*) detail

RLADON GDOG NUT
BALDON

DOLL

Moses Ogden **Animal Figure with Human Face** ca. 1890-1910, maple, 14"H x 23"W x 6"D
(left) Moses Ogden **Figure of a Woman** ca. 1890-1910, maple, fiber hair, 26"H x 13"W x 8"D
These figures are from "Moses Ogden's Wonderland" in Angelica, NY.

Eddie Arning **Untitled (Coppertone Girl)** ca. 1970, craypas on paper, 18 3/4"H x 24 3/4"W

Eddie Arning **Untitled (Swimmer on Green)** ca. 1970, craypas on paper, 21 3/4"H x 28"W

Topsy-Turvy Doll ca. late 19th - early 20th C., carved wood with polychrome, 16"H x 5"W x 3"D
(right) **Head of Scarecrow** ca. late 19th - early 20th C., carved wood with polychrome and metal, 13"H x 7"W x 16"D

Joseph Yoakum **Aranson Bay** 1966, colored pencil, watercolor and pen on paper, 12"H x 18"W

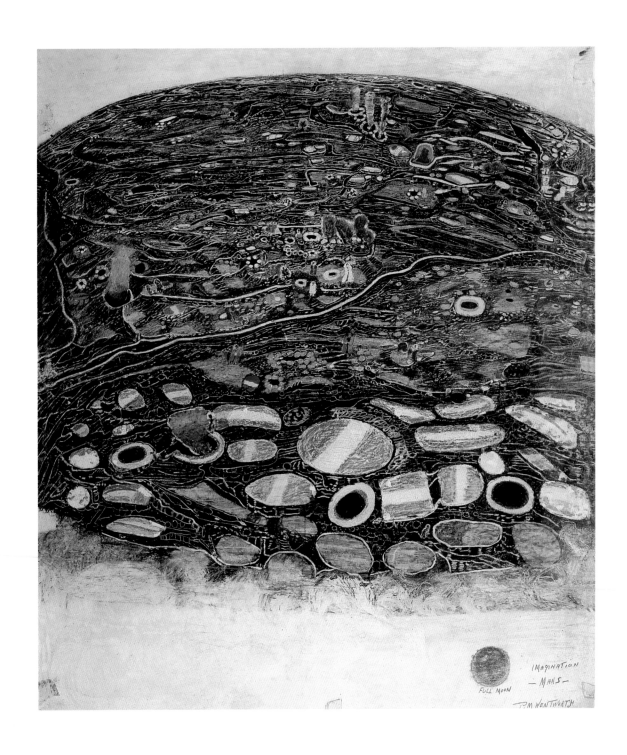

P.M. Wentworth **Imagination Mars** 1940, colored pencil and collage on paper, 25 1/2"H x 29 1/2"W

Bill Traylor **Untitled (Fighting Dogs)** ca. 1939-42, poster paint and graphite on cardboard, 18"H x 25 1/2"W

Bill Traylor **Untitled (Spread-Legged Drinker)** ca. 1939-42, poster paint and graphite on cardboard, 9 1/8"H x 13 5/8"W

Justin McCarthy **Beach Fashions** 1962, oil on board, 23 1/2"H x 47"W
(right) Drossos P. Skyllas **Untitled (Snow Scene)** 1950-60, oil on canvas, 32"H x 24"W

D. P. SKyllas

Articulated Mannequin from New England, late 19th - early 20th C., wood with polychrome and glass eyes, 70"H x 18"W x 12"D
(right) detail

Calliope Figure late 19th - early 20th C., wood with polychrome, fabric and leather, 48"H x 13"W x 2 1/2"D

Morton Bartlett **Waving Girl** ca. 1950-60, carved and painted plaster with fiber hair, 32 1/4"H x 6"W x 4"D

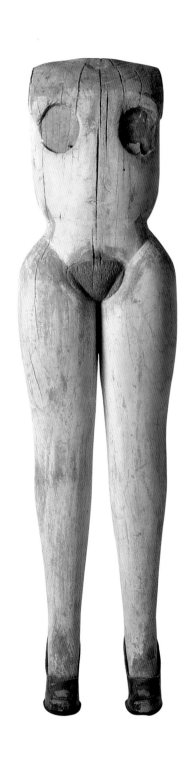

Display Mannequin ca. 1940s, wood with polychrome, 51"H x 12 1/2"W x 12"D

Raymond Coins **Carved Figure** ca. 1980, wood, 62"H x 15 3/4"W x 4"D

Morris Hirshfield **American Beauty** 1942, oil on canvas, 48"H x 40"W
(left) **Two Ton Tessie** ca. 1925-30, paint on canvas, 71"H x 60"W

Laura Craig McNellis **Untitled (Two Figures)** 1982, tempera on paper, 21"H x 28"W

Laura Craig McNellis **Untitled (Yellow Dress)** 1982, tempera on paper, 21"H x 27 1/2"W

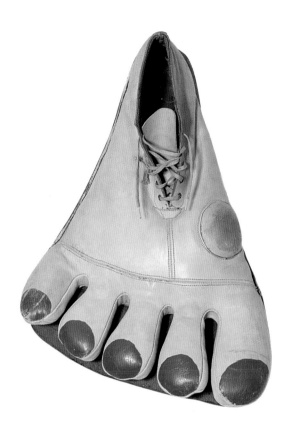

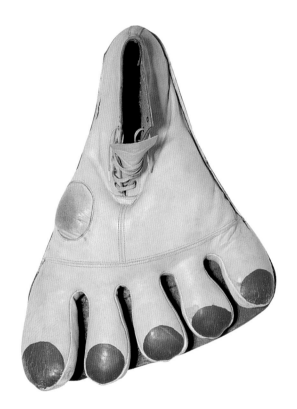

Clown Shoes for Dan "Papa" Kerr of Ringling Bros. ca. 1930-40, 18"H x 11"W x 4"D each
(right) **Collection of Lunch Boxes** from 1945-80, metal and vinyl with lithographed surfaces,
average size 8 1/2"H x 6 3/4"W x 4"D

Six Knockdown Carnival Heads ca. 1920, wood with polychrome and moveable eyes, 19"H x 7 1/2"W x 1 1/2"D each
(right) P.W. McAdam **Portrait of A Black Man** 1925, fired clay with brown slip glaze, 16"H x 8 1/2"W x 10"D

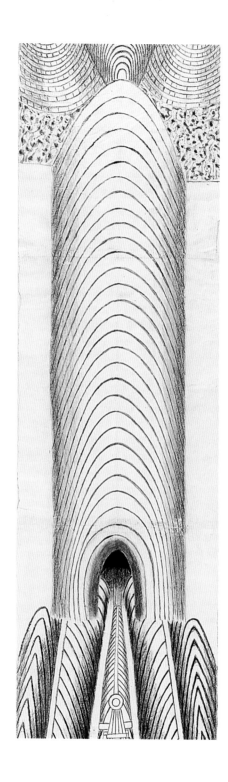

Martin Ramirez **Untitled (Tunnel with Train)** ca. 1950-55, pencil on paper, 71"H x 17"W
(*right*) **Life Guard Training Figure** ca. 1920-25, wood with metal and paint, 38"H x 16"W x 8 1/2"D

INDEX

Known artist names are listed in captions. All other works are Anonymous.

Kitsch Room Installation